Narcissistic Abuse

Recovery

The Complete Guide to Recover From Emotional

Abuse, Identify Narcissists, and Overcome

Abusive Relationships

Linda Hill

Linda Hill

Linda Hill

Table of Contents

Your Included Bonus

Get Your Setting Boundaries Cheat Sheet and Stop People Pleasing Guide For Free

This complimentary cheat sheet will make it simple for you to set boundaries with others in your life and protect your personal space. You will have practice scenarios and examples on what to do and say. In this guide, you will learn:

- New boundary setting skills by responding to different, real life scenarios.

- Proper responses to make in situations such as work and relationships.

- How to respond to people who are violating your personal space.

- 5 Must-do things when communicating your boundaries with others so they don't cross them.

Additional bonus: In addition to the above, the **Stop People Pleasing** guide will be included.

Visit here:
LindaHillBooks.com/setboundaries

QR Code:

Introduction

When a toxic person can no longer control you,
they will try to control how others see you. The
misinformation will feel unfair, but stay above it,
trusting that other people will eventually see the
truth just like you did.
–Jill Blakeway

Picture, if you can, a friend who has found their dream partner. The partner has most of the traits anyone else hopes for in an ideal mate: confidence, attentiveness, charm, and intelligence. As an observer of the friend with their partner, something may not feel quite right.

The partner may seem loud, dominating the conversation, or even speaking for the friend, even when conversation is directed to them. The attention that was noted as sweet initially seems more obsessive-based as the partner keeps track of every move the friend makes. The friend, who once had a boisterous and gregarious personality, now seems quiet, insecure, self-conscious, and guarded, hinting that they may be mistreated in some way. But without any obvious signs of abuse, no one intervenes. This is what a narcissistic abusive relationship looks like from the outside, and why narcissists are able to continue their behavior.

The worst part is that the victims in these sorts of relationships are either in deep denial that the problem is within the narcissist, or they've been made to believe all fault is theirs. The situation is not unlike being held in headlock with a muffle on, being forced to stay in a relationship that is completely one-sided. And even when the victim gathers enough courage to reach out to someone, they often aren't believed, which keeps the victim under a controlling thumb.

This form of abusive relationship is one of the most difficult to end and to recover from because the very core of a person has been damaged, and it's not discriminatory in any way. It doesn't care about gender, race, religion, social status or any other category people are put into. Narcissists exist in every area of life, and so do their targets. Worst yet, victims actually believe they'll never do any better, keeping them in that invisible headlock without a fight. But it doesn't have to be that way.

Those who are living with, healing and recovering from, or getting past the debilitating effects of being in a toxic relationship need the empowerment of information, which is the focus of this book. Understanding the mindset of a narcissist, their personality traits, and their effects on those around them gives victims a new perspective of what they endured as well as a renewed sense of self. It's also a way to recognize the warning signs in future potential relationships so as not to repeat the cycle.

This book doesn't shed a sympathetic light on the abuser, nor is the focus helping you figuring out whether or not you are in this kind of relationship, although you'll be given some tips on how to tell if you're unsure. The focus is on gaining insight to build up your strength to remove yourself from the relationship, the tools you need to rebuild yourself from the inside out, tips for not being drawn back in, then maintaining your new life the way you deserve to live. You're already aware that something isn't right. Your gut is rarely wrong. The point is to get you through and past the damage that's been done and rebuild your life from the inside out.

And we'll guide you through each step.

CHAPTER 1

What You Really Want to Know About Narcissists

Relationships with narcissists are held in place by the hope of a 'someday better', with little evidence to support it will ever arrive.

–Ramani Durvasula

If you already know your partner has a narcissistic personality, you're somewhat of an expert on how difficult a relationship with them can be. Maybe you are aware of what they're about, but you can seem to get them to leave and they won't let you walk away. Perhaps you see who they are and what they're doing to you, but you aren't sure how to let go. Or you have managed to walk away, but you're worried you'll either go back or that you'll never find anyone better. These are all valid concerns, which is why we're starting at square one with getting your life back.

The term *narcissism* is used so often it's true meaning gets confused. It's most commonly related to people who have strong personalities, whose confidence borders on arrogance. Those individuals need to dominate the conversation even if the topics aren't their strongest areas, and their egos influence their need to be the center of attention. Although many of these behaviors sound similar to a narcissist's personality, there are important differences that set them apart. This will be discussed in more detail later in the chapter.

Understanding the thought process of narcissists will also be touched on. This may trigger the question, "Why would I want to get into the head of someone like *that*?" but having this knowledge definitely puts the victim at an advantage. Knowing how they operate will enable you to be in control of your responses, taking away their power that they need to feel. Not only will this give you the courage to leave the toxic relationship, it will strengthen you from allowing the narcissist to lure you back.

Finally, in relation to the above point, we'll cover some possible explanations of how they became the way they are. As pointed out in the Introduction, we aren't trying to give sympathy to them when they never displayed any empathy for anyone else. Knowing the why of where they got their personality from will put your guard up whenever you sense their manipulative ways or when they try pushing familiar guilt buttons.

By the end of this chapter, you'll be more aware of what you've been dealing with and, maybe, even starting to feel a tiny bit more empowered.

Narcissism 101

To some degree, most individuals display traces of narcissism occasionally. When you think about it, children are by nature narcissistic in that they expect their needs and wants met regardless of convenience. They also want everyone's attention, and work pretty hard to get it. But children quickly learn that such behavior, and level of expectations from others, isn't just rude, it's also unrealistic. They do grow out of it eventually. Those who don't, and never learn more appropriate behavior, carry it through to adulthood.

Narcissism can be initially misinterpreted as merely having strong self-confidence in terms of who they are, what they do, and where they intend to go in life. In this sense, these people could be just mentally tough with a clear path to their achievement goals, channeling that narcissistic tendency more into ambition. The concern is when the self becomes the focus over their goals, even at the cost of other people's wants and needs. And it's at this point it branches off into a personality disorder, rather than a person who's simply secure in who they are.

Narcissistic Personality Disorder (NPD) is defined by the traits they display that revolve around their exaggerated view of self-importance. Specific traits that are strongly related to the narcissistic personality individual include:

- Grandiose perspective of their accomplishments,

talents, and capabilities

- Display perfectionism in every area of their lives, and expect it from others

- Need of constant attention and admiration, and no matter how much they receive it never seems to be enough

- Focus on superficial things (e.g. appearance, possessions, social status, etc.)

- Expectation of special treatment, even when it's not deserved

- Using manipulation and lying to get what they want, even if it means exploiting or taking advantage of others for their own wants

- Deficit in their ability to regulate their self-esteem

- Lack of emotional connection with others, and only associate with people they consider to be close to their own status

- Lack of respect for personal boundaries

- Lack of empathy

- Lack of accountability for their actions, and negative reaction to criticism

It may be surprising to know that deep beneath all of the facades, those with narcissistic personalities are actually insecure to the point of being self-loathing, which is why they work so hard for attention. And it could be why they treat others beneath them because that's how they may see themselves.

Under the umbrella of narcissism, there are four main categories that individuals can be specifically grouped into, based on what their focuses are. The traits listed above are seen in every category of narcissism. The main difference among these is how they express personality traits.

1. **Classic:** This group is the stereotypical narcissists who openly and unapologetically display the above personality traits. They don't see how their behavior is wrong or hurtful, and will actually point the finger elsewhere, deflecting all blame or wrongdoing on others.

2. **Vulnerable:** These individuals are also known as "closet narcissists" because although they still have beliefs of superiority, they are more introverted and avoid the spotlight. Usually, they attach themselves to those who are considered popular and already receive special treatment, rather than actively seeking it out themselves. They get attention by playing the victim or through false generosity. In other words, they don't give from the heart, they do it for the attention it gives them.

3. **Communal:** This one is a little sneakier to spot until you look at the person closely. These people seem to be strong advocates in the community or with specific charities but, in reality, they aren't supporting a cause for humanitarian reasons but more for praise and acknowledgement. Underneath it all, such a person is trying to feed their misguided sense of self.

4. **Malignant:** Of all main categories, this group of narcissists are the most toxic and ruthless. These individuals are highly manipulative and seemingly

get pleasure from exploiting others. This group is aggressive, controlling, deceitful, and will do anything to dominate. Worst of all, they feel no sense of remorse for anything they do.

Under each of these main categories, there are a few subtypes of narcissists depending on how their actions are viewed or experienced by others. Here's a rundown of the subtypes:

1. **Overt:** This group practices methods that are out in the open for everyone to see. The classic and communal groups are always overt.

2. **Covert:** These narcissists are so good at hiding what they do, it makes it difficult for those in a relationship with them to convince others of the truth. They're sneaky and passive-aggressive in their approach and are able to manipulate without another person's awareness at first. The vulnerable group is always covert. Because of the very nature of what they do and their high lack of

empathy and remorse, those in the communal group can be either overt or covert.

3. **Cerebral:** The title hints at brain functioning, but individuals in this group see their intellect as superior—making them believe they're more intelligent than everyone else. They monopolize the conversation, constantly prove how much they know, and interrupt when others try speaking.

4. **Somatic:** Individuals in this group are focused on their bodies, and judge others by their outward appearance. They are very likely to seek partners they can use as "shiny objects" to boost their visibility and popularity. They obsess about weight, physique, looks, and will criticize their partner—or others—for not meeting their standards.

People in these categories can also be included in any of the four major groupings.

5. **Inverted:** This subtype only relates to vulnerable or covert groups. These individuals are the

wounded victims who blame everyone else for what they've gone through. They attach themselves to other narcissists to feel exceptional, and these people are most likely to have developed their personality from childhood trauma.

6. **Sadistic:** These individuals are strictly under the malignant main category. Those in this subtype tend to be compared to sociopathic or psychopathic mindsets in that they take great pleasure in other people's pain. They thrive on humiliating, hurting and completely destroying other people's self-worth, and this mindset can even trickle into their sexual practices.

7. **Spiritual:** These individuals tend to display a "holier than thou" mindset, and use religion and spirituality to shame others or justify their treatment of others.

It's clear that narcissists have traits from each of these individual categories, but sometimes the focus is specifically on one area based on what's most important to them.

How Do Narcissists Become the Way They Do?

There doesn't seem to be a solid, proven reason how narcissistic personalities develop in some people but not in others. There are some genetic and environmental influences, but nothing absolute. Studies of the areas of the brain in charge of processing emotions, empathy, and certain cognitive functions have shown some deterioration or lack of development for those with this personality disorder (Psycom, 2022). Pretty much, then, we aren't born with personality disorder, but they develop in childhood through experience, genes, and what they're surrounded by within each of their environments (e.g. school, friends, family, etc.).

An important point to remember is that just because a young person expresses certain narcissistic traits doesn't mean they'll develop a disorder. It could be traits typical of their age group (e.g. focusing on the self). Bearing these points in mind, here are a few other possible reasons narcissists become the way they do:

- Developing a insensitive disposition at a young age

- Absorbing manipulative tactics from caregivers, siblings, or friends

- Being overly praised for good behavior and highly belittled for bad behavior

- Unclear boundaries or expectations

- Unrealistically praised

- Experiences of trauma, neglect, abandonment, or abuse in childhood

- Inconsistent or unreliable caregiving

- Highly overindulged by those around them growing up

- Unrealistic focus placed on looks, body image, or capabilities

You now have a clear definition of narcissism, their personality traits and possible reasons for how they developed their undesirable personality traits. The next chapter will focus on the tactics narcissists practice to stay in control of others (especially those they have intimate relationships with), and important points on what to do and *not* do when dealing with them.

Chapter 2

The Narcissist's Tactics to Control

You can't force someone to respect you, but you can refuse to be disrespected.
–Mohammad Rishad Sakhi

The reason for understanding the ins and outs of the narcissist's personality is so those closest to them know what they're dealing with. For those who have dealt with the toxic behavior long enough, there will be a deeper level of knowledge that will help protect you from any further hurt. For those who are new to a relationship with such a person, you now have solid information to either risk a move forward with your new partner, or to remove yourself before you get too involved.

It may seem counterproductive—in a way—to do deep research on the narcissist in your life. Aren't we doing exactly what they want us to do? Isn't making them our whole focus what they crave? On the surface, it may feel that way, but, first, they don't know you're gathering information for your benefit unless you tell them. Second, you aren't doing what they expect you to do because the information you're getting is to get away from them and to heal from their abusiveness, not to inflate to inflate their ego.

With that premise in mind, this chapter will open up the different tactics narcissists use to try getting you under their thumb. Again, although the terms themselves may not be familiar, the definitions of them might be. Recognize these tactics, name them, and stop them from continuing.

It's easy to fall prey both to their strategies, as well as to be lured back into them once you've been courageous enough to end the relationship. Once you recognize those strategies, you then have to arm yourself with inner power to know how to respond. Narcissists continue their toxic behavior because they're allowed to.

When they're faced with someone who won't fall for their charms, but also understands how to fight them, the narcissist will back off. They'll lose interest pretty quickly with a person they have to work too hard to get attention from.

That being said, an important side note needs to be made.

Although most narcissists won't waste their time with a person they can't control, those who fall in the sadistic mindset are more likely than others not to let go as easily. This group is more likely to stalk, make the victim look like the bad person, or attack the victim's good nature or reputation just to twist the knife of pain. Remember they get a lot of pleasure from another's suffering so any retaliation on the victim's part won't be let go. But don't despair. There is both light and protection.

In the final section of the chapter, we'll discuss whether the narcissist can change and when to accept when they won't. This is a tough realization because it also means accepting that you are a victim of abuse, and the next chapter will guide you through that.

The Narcissist's Dysfunctional Coping Methods

This chapter kicks off with the different controlling ways a narcissist shields their precious ego. They do this through practicing several forms of dysfunctional coping methods to hook, keep, and control their partners or others they allow close to them. If victims don't see these methods initially, they should identify them as soon as possible when the narcissist's spell starts to wear off.

Once the victim can see and label these methods, they can then use the suggestions provided in this book not only to control their reactions, but also revert the responsibility back on the narcissist. Know that it's easier to recognize the tactics than it is to effectively respond to them initially. It's important that if one isn't strong enough to fight back at first, to at least be consciously aware of what's happening. This is the first important step in stopping the toxic treatment that you'll use to draw from during your healing process.

The following are the most common tactics the narcissist turns to maintain their control:

- **Love-Bombing:** Before the narcissist can even get close enough to pull any tricks, they have to get the person of their focus to trust them. Love-bombing may actually seem innocent and flattering at first, but be on guard. The idea behind it is to overwhelm with presents, surprises, and other signs of affection as ways to—hopefully—spark interest in wanting to spend more time with the bomber. It may not seem obvious initially to the recipient but these are acts of manipulation to earn trust. So, how would the recipient know when the intentions are genuine, and when they're being snowed by a narcissist? From their perspective, they're watching how you respond in your world, then shower you with attention and gifts based on what makes you happiest. But all the showering of affection comes at a great cost. This is how love-bombing should look to the recipient:

○ Things are happening way too fast for comfort. A relationship takes time but it should be rather alarming when a person is talking about love, having a family, and marriage not too long after meeting.

○ The bomber will come across as extreme and over-the-top in their approach.

○ They always tell you what you want to hear, even regarding your insecurities, with no sense of genuinity.

○ If they think you're not responding positively, they'll take steps back until they hit the right response. Remember that they aren't concerned about the sincerity of their approach, only how they look.

○ One big hint is that they may be treating you really well but they aren't so kind to anyone else. Many victims miss this because of how good the attention makes them feel but it should be a neon sign that they'll be treated in the same way before too long.

○ They'll start asking prying questions about any hard times you've gone through, and really press for you to be candid. This is another huge red flag because these kinds of things should come up naturally after strong, mutual trust has been established. The narcissist is just pocketing ammo for future use.

- **Gaslighting:** This tactic is definitely felt before the recipient realizes it's being done to them. This is one of the highest forms of manipulation and leaves the victim confused and doubting their own sanity. When it's allowed to go on long enough, the victim loses their ability to trust themselves or their own perceptions of what's real. And, again, there are different ways a toxic person tries to gaslight someone:

○ They tell you that you aren't remembering something right or that you're plain out wrong when you know you are right.

- They make you feel that your thoughts and feelings don't matter to anyone else, either.

- They withhold information, then act like they don't know what you're talking about.

- They give you the silent treatment.

- They make you doubt your own thoughts by questioning the validity of them.

- They justify their actions because it's for your own good.

- They deny something ever happened.

- **Projection:** This is the act of one person putting uncomfortable feelings or accountability onto someone else. A narcissist won't take responsibility for their actions and will go out of their way to make someone else take onus for their bad doings in very damaging and cruel ways.

- **Deflection:** Anyone who has tried winning an argument with a narcissist is well-versed in this strategy. This is the act of avoiding an issue or problem by talking around it until the initial subject matter is lost or forgotten. Have you ever walked away from a conversation feeling lost, confused or at a loss of what point you were even trying to make in the first place? The narcissist deflected the conversation as a way to avoid accountability.

- **Distortion:** This is a tactic where the narcissist twists the truth around in such a way, you actually doubt yourself, even though the facts were clear in your mind before confronting the narcissist. They are a master of deceit and use a variety of methods to distort your reality:

  ○ They're always trying to prove themselves as being right.

  ○ They form a conclusion based on one incident and generalize it to everything else.

  ○ They jump to conclusions based on what they think rather than on facts.

  ○ They'll either magnify the importance of

specific details, or minimize or completely disregard them.

○ They often put unrealistic obligations on others using the 'should' statements.

○ They play the victim, even when the subject matter has little to do with them.

○ They play the emotional card, overshadowing any sense of logical thinking.

○ Not only do they expect others to change to meet their needs, they also believe they're in control of themselves and everyone/everything around them.

• **Triangulation:** This is when the narcissist recruits another person to side with them to support their endeavors in harming the victim. This is most often done as a form of punishing the victim either for not doing what's expected of them or when they finally see the light and end the toxic relationship.

- **Splitting:** This is a form of black-and-white thinking with no other options.

- **Negging:** This is a form of emotional manipulation where the person gives backhanded compliments to elicit self-doubt and slowly tear away at the receiver's self-esteem.

Sometimes these sorts of strategies are done so subtly that the target person isn't even aware it's happening until they're in pretty deep. Even at that, though, one should still be able to sense something isn't right based on the way they feel. Gut feelings are very powerful and rarely wrong.

The Do's and Don'ts for Responding to a Narcissist

After the discussion in this chapter, it's clear that communication with them is challenging. It's difficult to reason with someone who won't see past their own wants and how they can benefit from everything and everyone around them. The advantage you now have is understanding not only what to watch out for in terms of their personality, but also the way they carry out their mission in controlling what goes on in their environment.

This section will go a bit further in the "must knows" to have on your side. We're going to talk about ten *don'ts* in dealing with a narcissist and why they're important to know about. This gives a victim more power to stop them in their tracks, and keep them at bay. We'll end the chapter with seven *do's* when facing conflict with the narcissist and how to stop the argument before they have a chance to try one of their tactics.

First, here are the *don'ts* in dealing with a narcissist in general:

1. **Never underestimate them.** This is a group of individuals who are never satisfied on any level. It's clear that they have developed a huge sense of self that they don't see any other person matching and certainly not surpassing. That being said, they know exactly what to say to get what they want. Be on guard and second-guess every word they say, especially any hints of their willingness to

change.

2. **Empathy isn't going to happen.** Lack of empathy is one of the staple traits of any category of narcissistic personality. In order to feel empathy, a person has to be willing to see a situation through another person's eyes as well as understand that other people are worthy of and deserve compassion. A narcissist can't give what they don't feel. Rather than trying to make them understand this, focus more on honoring and respecting yourself by staying behind your boundaries (this will be discussed in more detail in a later chapter).

3. **Never give them ammo.** Guard your thoughts, feelings, and other areas of your inner self carefully. Anything you reveal to them, they will use against you in some way.

4. **There's more to them than meets the eye.** Narcissists work very hard to emit the facade of perfection and superiority. The irony is that underneath all the masks, they actually feel exactly

opposite to the image they portray. As fellow humans, we can feel compassion for them, but in no way should we be taken in by their tactics.

5. **Display your best poker face.** A narcissist sees everyone as either an enemy or someone to use, and they save their absolute worst for those they allow closest to them. No matter what they say or do, never give them the satisfaction of knowing they got to you. That's their main goal, don't help them make it easier.

6. **Don't expect their support.** Narcissists have no loyalty to others. If a person doesn't meet their needs or desires, they're tossed aside. Expecting this from a person who is in everything for themselves, is setting you up for tremendous hurt.

7. **You don't owe them explanations or justifications.** If anything, they owe this to their victims, but it shouldn't be expected. Trying to explain or justify feelings to a narcissist is another way to hand them ammo. They don't communicate, they won't reason and they don't

care about working out issues. All they care about is winning.

8. **Never minimize or downplay their behavior.** As an extension of the above point, just because there's no point in trying to get them to listen to how their words, actions, and behavior hurt, it doesn't mean you should minimize it to yourself. It's crucial that you comfort yourself with the fact that they have no right to make others feel that way, and you won't allow their inflictions to get under your skin. Your self-worth is precious and valuable, and they shouldn't be allowed to damage it.

9. **Don't expect accountability.** This point has been touched on earlier, but understanding that they won't take onus for their behavior saves a lot of time and energy. If you want to verbalize their responsibility for their actions for ease of mind, that's certainly appropriate. But don't expect them to take what you say to them to heart.

10. **Don't try to get even.** As tempting as it may be

to beat them at their own game or to get even, it isn't worth the energy. The narcissist has been doing what they do their entire lives, and are experts in the field of pain and hurt. Going up against them at their own game is like a lightweight boxer going up against the heavyweight world champion. The best way to fight back in your own way is to stick to your values and be true to yourself.

Some of the *don'ts* may seem obvious but for those who are tangled right in the middle of a narcissist's web, or who are new in this sort of relationship, it's imperative to stay informed and protect themselves.

The *do's* are meant to help you with the subject focus in the next chapter. The focus will be on acknowledging the effect of narcissistic abuse on overall health. For those who see what's happening to them, it will be an extra boost to face up to the abuser and the strength to get away from them. For those still not quite sure, the information will open the door to realization and, hopefully, acceptance. There's nothing more important than your health, and you can't go on very long when it's impaired.

These tips will arm you with the courage you need when you face and stand up to the narcissistic abuser. The manipulation will continue even at the point where they know their tactics will no longer keep you around, so be strong.

Here are some *do's* when dealing with confrontation with a narcissist:

- **Let go of blame.** As you know by now, trying to make the narcissist take responsibility for their part in things going wrong is a waste of energy and emotion. They aren't going to admit to anything that makes them appear opposite to the image of perfection they believe they are.

- **Empathize with their feelings.** Many individuals may think, "Why should I give them a shred of empathy when they have none for anyone else?" Sometimes the best way to end the argument faster, or at least deflate it, is to relate to their feelings. This may be a tough one to put into play, but they'll respond better to a gentler approach.

- **Let them think you're in it together.** Using 'I' or 'you' singles each of you out, which never goes off well with a narcissist, so opting for the 'we' language is a wise move. They will be angry enough that you've confronted them or even defended yourself, but using 'we' reminds them it involves both of your behavior.

- **Put yourself first.** This is a difficult thing to put into practice when you've been forced to put someone else before your own wants and needs. Keep yourself in front and don't give them the power to bring you back into their web.

- **Ignore the bait.** When the narcissist is confronted, they'll attempt to turn everything around on you, adding insults, blame, or belittling into play. Of course, a natural reaction is to jump into defense mode, but that's exactly what they want. The best thing to do is ignore the insults, tune out the bait, and stay focused on the main issue.

- **It's okay not to get an apology.** We've already discussed that they don't feel remorse or empathy, both of which you need to feel in order to offer a sincere apology. Plain and simple, they can't offer something that they neither feel or relate to.

- **When all else fails, feed their ego.** If you aren't able to find your breakaway within any of these scenarios, practice the art of distraction. They love talking about themselves, and love being given the opportunity to prove they know more than anyone else. If changing the subject doesn't work, try asking for their advice. This is a last resort tip to at least put the never ending circle of argument to an end.

The discussions will better prepare you to absorb the next chapter's focus on recognizing, dealing with, and calling the narcissist out for their abusive behavior. It's time to take the first step in halting the toxic relationship and preparing to head down the road of recovery.

CHAPTER 3

Recognizing and Stopping Narcissistic Abuse

It's okay to speak up for yourself, be assertive, and refuse disrespect. It doesn't make you aggressive. It makes you someone who is setting healthy boundaries.
–Karen Salmansohn

The most difficult aspect of being in an abusive relationship, no matter what category it may fall in, is the realization that you have been abused. Acceptance is vital in being able to build the courage to end the relationship, embracing the reconstruction of your self-worth in recovery, and maintaining the resilience to move forward in healing. *Acceptanc*e doesn't mean accepting what's happened to you, it means making yourself conscious of the abuse so you can make positive changes.

This chapter will be the peak of the book. Armed with information about the narcissist—their personality and making their tactics easier to point out—will make it easier to start turning the tables around. It's important for the targets of a narcissist's venomous ways to realize that the treatment you endure isn't normal, you don't deserve it, and it does more than make you feel bad about yourself (which, in itself, is enough). Abuse, especially when it affects every area of your well-being, hurts your overall health. It can have lingering effects on you mentally, including trauma from which you may never completely heal. Finally, because the abuse harms the very core of your being and self-worth, it may take a long time to be able to trust or even see yourself the same way.

Should one person be permitted to have so much power that they can destroy another being so completely? We say no! And you will too.

In this chapter, you'll become consciously aware of how deeply the narcissist's abuse has impaired you. You'll be able to recognize the signs so that you'll be able to counteract those responses with more positive ones. You'll learn the best way to confront your abuser, then cut ties with them. And in case you need a bit of extra incentive, we'll outline exactly how that person has interfered with your overall functioning. It's time to realign the defragmented areas of your mind, body, and spirit selves; which starts with taking back the power the abuser believes they have over you.

This may be a tough discussion for some of you. It may be a good idea to contact your primary healthcare provider in getting through certain points, especially those focusing on physical or mental health. Knowing both of these areas have gone through a great deal of trauma, having some insight and care to make sure you come out of it all on top is a wise choice.

Finally Seeing the Light

All forms of abuse tend to follow a specific and clear

pattern that stems from, and revolves around, control. The narcissist starts slow and steady to draw their target in, showers the person with attention and shiny things to get the target where they want them, then starts to reveal their true self.

It should be pointed out here that narcissistic personalities and abuse aren't tied together in every situation. Not all abusers have narcissistic personalities, even though they too can be controlling and manipulative. And people can possess some of the personality traits of a narcissist, but not be abusive. That point made, it doesn't give *anyone* the right to hurt others for their own gain. And here are the main signs to recognize when you're in a narcissistic relationship:

1. **They were perfect… initially.** We've discussed this one, but it's worth mentioning again. A narcissist wants you to believe they're totally into you and put you on a pedestal. Once they have you, though, they stop trying as hard and you end up being the one working to keep them.

2. **Others don't see the narcissist the way you do.** It's hard enough to see it yourself, but when those around you, especially *their* friends and family, make excuses for them, you start doubting yourself even more. Stick to what you see.

3. **They're making you look bad.** In order to maintain their facade of perfection, they make you look like a bad person. Usually this involves spreading rumors, criticizing you behind your back, or creating lies you supposedly told. The worst part is that when you try rectifying the situation, or laying the blame where it should belong, the narcissist uses your defense to back their own lies. It's frustrating because the generous, wonderful person they displayed initially is what those around you still see, even if you see them for who they really are.

4. **You feel symptoms of anxiety and/or depression.** The toxic person may have caused you to worry about not acting the way you're expected to, or that you haven't done something right or good enough. In making this person your

entire world, you may lose sleep, have no interest in things you used to or have developed a, "What's the point?" attitude. You essentially absorb all of the negative talk and treatment so deeply, you believe it all. This is a dangerous mindset to be in so if you feel you're going any steps down this path, seek outside help as soon as possible.

5. **You have unexplained physical ailments.** It's not surprising that when you internalize a great deal of negativity, you begin to feel unwell. Some common symptoms that aren't related to any ongoing condition might be: changes in appetite, stomach issues, body aches, insomnia, and fatigue. These are typical bodily responses to stress, but if they intensify or become chronic, see a physician as soon as you can.

6. **You feel alone.** Also a common symptom of abuse. If things are really wrong, the narcissist may have isolated you from friends or family either by things they've done themselves or by making you believe no one is there for you.

7. **You freeze.** When you emotionally remove yourself from the abuse, you're freezing. It's a coping mechanism to reduce the intensity of the way you're being treated by numbing out the pain.

8. **You don't trust yourself even with simple decisions.** When your self-esteem has been crushed through devaluing and criticism, it's no wonder you can't make decisions. If you're also being gaslighted, it adds another layer of self-doubt.

9. **You can't make boundaries.** The narcissist doesn't have any, nor do they respect them, which is why it's difficult to keep them away even after you've managed to get away. Setting boundaries will be discussed in greater detail in an upcoming chapter.

10. **You lost touch with the real you.** The person you become when with a narcissistic abuser is very different from the person you were before you got involved with them. They've turned you into who they want you to be, making you feel lost and

insecure with no sense of true purpose.

11. **You never feel like you do anything right.** We touched on this briefly above, but this is one of the main signs of narcissistic abuse. Looking at the big picture, you may be constantly blamed when things go wrong even when it isn't your fault. You may do something exactly the way they tell you to, but they still find fault with the results. It's similar to how a Private feels never knowing when the Drill Sergeant will find fault in their efforts.

12. **You walk on eggshells.** This happens when you try avoiding any sort of conflict, maltreatment or backlash by going above and beyond to make the abuser happy.

This list of signs can make it clear that ignoring what the narcissistic abuser is doing to you can result in long-term mental, physical and emotional effects. To say the least, that isn't fair, and no person should ever feel they should be permitted to have control over another. So, what can you do to stop the train from going to the point of no return?

In the last chapter, we discussed how to bring down the intensity level of an argument. Now we're going to share five ways to confront the narcissist about their abuse and come out relatively unscathed.

These are things to have under your belt in order to make and strengthen boundaries:

1. **Educate them.** To be blunt, narcissists aren't exactly in tune with their interpersonal or communication skills. Try using incentives or other motivators to get them to pay attention to how their behavior affects others. They may not empathize or seem to get what you're saying, but at least you can say you tried to look at it from your point of view.

2. **Understand your personal rights.** In order to demand being treated fairly and with respect, it's important to know what your rights are. You're allowed to say no, you have a right to your feelings, you are allowed privacy—and there are no wedding or relationship vows that say you are at the beck and call of your partner. When a

person has been abused for a long time, they may lack the confidence or self-esteem to take a stand on their rights. The more power they take back, though, the less the abuser has.

3. **Be assertive.** This is something that depends on confidence, and will take practice, but it's worth it. Being assertive means standing up for yourself and exuding pride in who you are.

4. **Put your strategies into play.** After the information you've absorbed so far, you have an advantage in that you are aware of your wants, what the narcissist demands, what you are able to do and those secret tiny areas you may have power over. Tap into these areas to put together your own strategies.

5. **Re-set your boundaries.** A boundary is an unseen line in the sand. It determines the point you won't allow others to cross over or they'll hurt you. These are non-negotiable and others must be aware of them and respect them. But you have to know what those lines are before making them

clear to others.

6. **Have consequences.** As an extension of the above point, if a person tries ignoring your boundaries, make sure you give a consequence. There doesn't need to be a threat, but more saying, "If you _____, we can't hang out/date/talk/etc." You're just saying that crossing the boundary hurts you so if they choose to disregard it, you choose not to accept that treatment.

The narcissist will not tolerate you standing up for yourself, but it's still important. The act of advocating for yourself will increase your self-confidence, self-esteem and self-worth. Then you'll be ready to recover and heal.

The Effects of Narcissistic Abuse on Your Overall Health

Several of the effects of narcissistic abuse were outlined above in the symptoms section. In this section, we're going to list some additional and specific effects that this abuse has on your overall health.

The effects of narcissistic abuse can vary based on the length of time the victim was exposed to it, as well as the severity level of the abuse. Here are some other ways this form of abuse can negatively impact your health:

- **Self-destructive behavior:** When someone has been in a controlling relationship long enough, they carry on with the feelings of shame and fault even after the relationship has ended. This can flow over into forms of self-harm and substance abuse to continue with what the abuser did to them.

- **Overly obliging:** Being forced to make the needs and wants of another person a number one priority from wake up until bedtime can result in extending the people-pleasing into other areas of your life.

- **Trust issues:** Being mentally abused to the point where a person doubts themselves, or doesn't even trust themselves or others, it can create severe trust issues. This can even lead to more severe concerns such as social anxiety. It instills mistrust of what others say, what they really mean and their sincerity.

- **Emotionally disconnected:** It's not uncommon to not understand how to emotionally respond to situations or people, or even express emotions at all.

- **Cognitive issues:** This can be the result of the ill-treatment itself or the physical symptoms impairing health. Lack of sleep can result in many of the symptoms listed earlier as can digestive issues. Additional concerns also include memory loss, inability to concentrate, losing focus performing basic tasks or "spacing out".

- **Inability to forgive the self:** Feelings of unworthiness, shame and blame dissipate over time they never completely go away. Similar to PTSD, one small trigger can be all it takes to relive the trauma. Another aspect of this is a damaged self-worth that causes us to not make an effort to reach goals or dreams, or we self-sabotage because we're convinced we don't deserve happiness or success.

Acknowledging that all you've gone through is *abuse*, and informing yourself with the effects it has had on your health, should be seen as a good thing.

Yes, it's difficult to look on the inside to see how significantly the abuse has hurt you. It should also be inspiring to know that you have the control and power in your hands to stop it, change your life and look ahead to a bright life coming.

That's the focus of our next chapter, which will guide you to the initial steps on your recovery path.

CHAPTER 4

Recovering From Narcissistic Abuse

I didn't leave because I stopped loving you. I left because the longer I stayed, the less I loved myself.

–Rupi Kaur

Hopefully after reading the previous chapter, you felt a sense of newfound inspiration to make the steps towards removing yourself from your toxic partner. If you've already chosen to leave, or convinced them to, you've already taken that very first baby step on your path to recovery and healing. If you haven't made the move yet, we'll share a few tips on preparing to get away as quickly and painlessly as possible. It's time to live your life the way you deserve to.

Once the plan is made to remove yourself from your abuser, the chapter discusses many tips to keep you moving along that road of recovery. Know that you no longer have to continue thinking no one will believe you, help you, or even be there for you. Yes, there will be those who side with the narcissist, but only because they're very good at their sabotage strategy, but not all witnesses are so easily swayed.

The next step is creating your recovery plan, including the very important support network. Then not only will you have tools and strategies to prepare for your recovery journey, but you'll also have a set plan for whenever your abuser slips into your thoughts and triggers emotions. Getting over an abusive relationship shares the same part of your brain in charge of keeping substance additions on the surface. The narcissist was your bad habit taking over your life and hurting you, so getting over them will take inner strength, perseverance, and willpower to resist their charms.

We'll start off with several crucial things you might not

have been told will happen while moving through your narcissist abuse recovery path. This will be a strong pull to lead you into the next chapter's focus of healing the inner self.

How to Leave a Narcissist, and Stay Away

Ending a toxic relationship with a narcissist is hard enough, but actually picking up and leaving that person will be one of the most difficult decisions you face—at the same time, it will also be one of the best and healthiest you make. But it will be much easier for you to let go than it will be for the narcissist, and they won't make it easy. In fact, some important questions may come to mind whether you're even making the right decision. And if there is a child involved, second thoughts about leaving may flood your brain even stronger.

The number one question to ask yourself, that isn't even on this short list coming up, is do you want your *child* to continue witnessing the toxic person's abusive behavior towards you? More importantly, do you want that person influencing your child to be the same way? Hopefully, your response is a big "no" to both of those questions.

Here are a few others to keep in mind before we remind you of the reasons you're better off without them:

- **What if I give them a chance to change. Is it possible?** The humanitarian response is anything is possible. But in the case of narcissists, the answer is no. They see nothing wrong with their behavior, blame you for any wrongdoing, and their treatment of you worsens the longer you stay in the relationship. That should be the strong, long form answer you need to stick to your decision.

- **What if they try calling/texting me?** They will because they don't like to lose. The best way to handle their attempts at contact is sticking to a strict "no contact" rule, which we'll discuss later. This is a rule you need to set in stone and not open the door a crack for them.

- **How do I co-parent with a narcissist?** This is a tough question that a therapist may be needed to work through with both parents. First, parenting is about cooperation and collaboration with every decision regarding the child's care. When one parent is incapable of these tasks, the situation may require some intervention. After all, in such a case the child isn't an object to fight over—they are a young person whose rights, needs, and care should be met. If the narcissist isn't willing to, or won't try to work with you; do what's best for the child, first and foremost.

- **How do I protect my child from being influenced or hurt by a narcissist?** Whether the person is a friend, relative, parent, teacher, or other person, children are tremendously influenced by those around them. If there are any signs that the child is experiencing the same maltreatment as you have, intervene immediately. Talk with your child and teach them the art of negotiation and fair treatment. Don't allow any abuse around them and don't lower yourself to the abuser's level by insulting them, putting them down, or otherwise openly expressing negative feelings. If you're showing your child the very best, non-conflictive behavior to deal with others, even when being influenced by the narcissist, then you're teaching them the right way to deal with adversity. It may not seem like it initially, but they do see and appreciate what you're doing. Down the road, it will be you they'll respect for handling things with grace.

- **What do I do if the narcissist parent gets custody of my child?** As hard as it is to believe, this could happen. All you can do as the estranged parent is make sure that the child isn't being manipulated, used to hurt you, or otherwise mistreated. Try reminding yourself that the situation isn't your fault, and try living the best life you can. Keep the lines of communication open with your child, and listen with empathy when you speak with them. This is something they may not be receiving from the other caregiver. Under no circumstances should you tolerate being abused or disrespected by your child and tell them so. Be sure to practice self-care (which we discuss in more detail in a later chapter) and surround yourself with loving, caring, and supportive people. Most of all, never give up hope. Don't let a day go by without reminding your child how much you love them.

Recovering from a toxic relationship isn't about putting all the blame on the abuser. It's more about dealing with the feelings that drew you to the person initially. It also includes becoming fully aware of the 'you' that was pushed aside during the course of that relationship. That means not focusing only on the pain that the person inflicted, but what the root of the pain is and healing that.

It's important at this point to remind yourself of all the *why's* for leaving. And just because that person doesn't plan to make your departure easy, you need to know you are stronger than you believe. Not every person in the same situation will follow their gut, stand firm behind their boundaries and forge ahead no matter how tough it seems. In addition to that, here are several things to remember to succeed in your getaway as safely as possible:

1. **No more chances.** You'd think a person who treated you unworthy of being with them would have no problem letting you go, right? Wrong. In fact, they may even initially beg you to stay, make promises to change, share their sob stories, or even go back to love-bombing you to change your mind. If you fall into their trap, though, it won't take long until they go right back to the way they were, or treat you even worse than they did before to punish you. Long story short? Don't give them any second (third, forth, etc.) chances. You've made your choice, they need to deal with it.

2. **Don't tell them you're leaving right away.** This may seem to contradict what's been said earlier, but delaying letting the abuser know when you're leaving may be a wise decision. In the best scenario, leaving when they aren't right there will alleviate a lot of drama, and they certainly don't need a set exact time and date of when you're planning to go. As with the points made above, the narcissist will do what they can to make you stay, not because they're fighting for your relationship but more because you have the nerve

to leave them. Protect yourself as much as you can.

3. **Don't give them the opportunity to spy on you.** This goes beyond changing passwords for all of your devices. You also have to make sure they can't track where you are or what you're doing. Log out of everything, change passwords, create a new email address, and make sure you don't have any sort of tracker on your phone. This may sound like overkill but it's better to be oversafe than vulnerable.

4. **Change your bank account.** If you never shared accounts, debt, or assets with the narcissist, they shouldn't be able to get to you through your bank. If you did share any sort of account with them, remove yourself from it, close it, or simply take what's yours and open your own account without them knowing.

5. **Reconnect with family and friends.** You may not have had contact with close friends or family for a long time as narcissists aren't open to their

partners having supportive relationships outside of their realm of control. You may be surprised that some of them may have known something wasn't right but didn't know how to intervene without making things worse. Good friends and family will always be there, even after a hiatus.

6. **Get rid of the other toxic people.** As an extension of the above point, not everyone will be as supportive. In fact, they may even side with the narcissist, believing their lies. As you walk out the door on the abuser, take the opportunity to get rid of the others with the same mindset. You don't need any more people like that around you.

7. **Once you leave, don't go back—for any reason.** We touched on the fact earlier that ending an abusive relationship is similar to breaking a habit, according to the brain. A habit is created by continuously doing something until you do it without thinking, and to break it requires a lot of work. Think of your narcissistic abuser as a habit that you need to break, including those cravings that try luring you back to it. It's done, over, and

there's no reason to go back.

8. **Throw away gifts or any love-bombing trinkets.** Let's go a step further. Gather up anything that reminds you of that person, and throw it all in the bin. You don't need any reminders of their presence and the actual motion of throwing things away is significant. Every part of them is gone from your space, allowing you to move forward.

9. **Face the trauma.** This may require either a person in your support network (to be touched on later), or a professional. To go on with your own life, throwing the abuser's things out may not be enough. You'll still be living with the scars. Face all that happened, all that was taken away, and ground yourself in healthy ways. Once you can do that, you're truly ready to completely let go.

10. **Make a list.** If the narcissistic abuser continues contacting you, or starts stalking you, record each and every time. This information will help you if you need to get a no-contact order or press

charges. Stalking is not only illegal, it's a breach of a person's basic rights.

11. **Report what happened to you.** This point and the last one are closely related. Many people never even go to the authorities or even tell their primary healthcare provider that they're being abused. If you're concerned about elevating the situation, the physician can at least refer you to resources that can help.

These are some of the things that we don't always think of when ending a toxic relationship and removing ourselves from the abuser. It's important to remember to protect yourself from all angles so the person holds no cards whatsoever. They've held onto them firmly long enough. The time has come for them to show their hand, and pay their dues.

Creating a Recovery Plan

Before jumping in and creating a recovery plan, it might be helpful to know a few facts that not many others either know, or do know but won't tell you, about the recovery process. These things are important in bringing up so the reason for creating your recovery plan makes more sense.

- **There aren't a set of steps to recovery.** Unlike recovering from substance abuse or other addiction, there are no set steps for recovering from an abusive relationship. Recovery isn't done in sequential steps, nor is it always linear. And there isn't an emphasis on specific steps—which could help people believe they're doing what they should be, when they should be. It can take a long time to heal from abuse, so give yourself the time you need.

- **Social media adds fuel to the fire.** There are some helpful platforms out there, and it's sometimes comforting when others post words of wisdom and personal experiences. Rather than tuning into random posts by strangers it's better to seek out posts made by professionals who have knowledge, training, and experience in narcissistic abuse.

- **Learn to trust yourself.** The mind games you

were put through can make you doubt your own sanity. In order for recovery to begin, you need to find ways to trust yourself again. Re-establishing your self-worth, self-esteem, and confidence—one baby step at a time will help you to slowly remove those negative tapes that play in your head.

- **You may never feel closure.** For many of us, closure marks the final ending of a situation, event, or experience that allows us to just let go. Closure can come about in many different ways depending on the individual. Those trying to move on in a new life after a crushing abusive relationship with a narcissist may simply want verification that everything that had happened wasn't their fault. Victims want the abuser to show some remorse for what they went through, which won't happen from a narcissist. That means finding the needed closure in a different way, and that's from within. The strength and courage it took to remove yourself from that level of abuse is powerful, and not a move that many others in the same situation are able to do. The closure you're looking for can be drawn from that, as well as knowing that you ended a highly toxic relationship by your own devices and creating a better self. That's something the narcissist can't take away from you.

- **Embrace the *right* help.** It is vital to surround yourself with people who support you in your recovery process. That means being open with your healthcare provider so they're able to guide you to healing your body properly. You absolutely need a therapist who has experience in and understanding of the narcissistic personality and their impact on other people. Unfortunately, there aren't a lot of therapists who are trained specifically in victims of narcissistic abuse. If you aren't able to find one with this focus, search for one recommended by your healthcare provider, other survivors of this form of abuse, therapists who deal with the ongoing symptoms you have (e.g. anxiety, depression, PTSD), or even a therapist who is an expert in Cognitive Behavioral Therapy (CBT) or trauma-informed therapy. Both of these work people through their trauma symptoms by learning better responses to triggers.

We'll be touching on the last point in greater detail in the next chapter, but these are important steps in creating your individual recovery plan. There are basically four steps in creating your recovery plan template that you can revise and update as you move further along your healing path.

Each person's view of their plan will be as individual as their situation is, but the base of it contains these basic sections:

Step One: Cut the Umbilical Cord From the Narcissist

At this point, some of you may have already accomplished this step, but it's added for those who haven't.

- Remove yourself out of denial and accept that what you're experiencing is abuse.

- Understand everything you can about the narcissistic personality and arm yourself with information. That gives some power back in your hands.

- Sever all communication or contact with the narcissist. If this isn't possible because the person is a family member or co-worker, learn low-contact strategies.

Step Two: Self-Care Is Priority #1:

Self-care—nurturing physical, mental, emotional and spiritual health—is the first thing to be tossed aside when having a relationship with a narcissist. This needs to be put back into place:

- Adjust your thinking from, "They want me to _____," or "If I don't _____ I'll pay for it," to "I need to _____ for *me*." It will be difficult initially to put yourself first, but that's what self-care is.

- Create an iron-clad support network consisting of professionals and trusted family and friends who will be your allies during your healing.

- Reconnect the areas of your whole self by

nurturing each of the areas of your overall health.

- Know who triggers memories or emotional vulnerability and limit any contact with those people.

Step Three: Daily Check-Ins With Your Inner Self

The point of this step is maintaining your end goal, ensuring that your perception of your world coincides with what you're doing to strengthen your inner self:

- Face every situation with honesty, accountability, and courage.

- Do a self check daily to make sure that your thoughts, feelings, reactions, and behaviors are on track. If there's anything amiss, take it as your challenge of the day to face and deal with effectively.

- Do a separate self check whenever you come across a person who either triggers memories from your abusive relationship, or who is toxic in some way.

Step Four: Strengthen Connection With Your Inner Self

These are points to maintain everything you've done up to this point, and to keep track of what's working and what needs adjustment:

- Let go of feelings of shame, guilt, or blame by forgiving yourself. You did all you thought you needed to to protect yourself, and you still are.

- Learn to let go of all feelings of hurt, and allow yourself to grieve the relationship. This point may seem odd to many, but you did spend a great deal of time with someone, and gave your heart to them. So although it was abusive, grief still needs to be dealt with: grief for what you gave up of yourself, grief for time lost to the abuser, or however grief looks and feels to you. Look at it, accept it, feel it, then let it go.

- Stay in tune with your inner voice and make sure everything it says to you is positive, loving, and inspiring. Whenever it starts playing more negative tapes, stop them by reminding yourself of all the good you're doing and that those tapes can no longer affect you.

- Examine your boundaries constantly. Are they clear enough? Do they need to be restructured? Do you need new ones? Have you removed the old ones that no longer work for you? Boundaries are extremely important both for what you accept as appropriate from others, and for what they're allowed to do to you. You came out of a relationship where boundaries were neither acknowledged or respected, so put those back up immediately and stay on top of them.

- Do not accept any form of toxicity in your new life under any circumstances. You don't need to be lured back into a world you turned your back on because it hurt you.

That is the recovery plan template in a nutshell. It may be very useful to have a journal or two to keep track of your progress, or even to write down thoughts or feelings. These things need to go somewhere, which is what therapy is good for. But journaling is a cleansing and safe way to put those thoughts, concerns, and emotions somewhere so you won't find maladaptive ways to cope.

In the next chapter, the discussion will focus on the importance of creating a solid support network, how to rebuild the inner self, and how to incorporate the mindset of mental toughness into your continued healing journey.

Chapter 5

Strengthening the Inner Self

A narcissist doesn't break your heart, they break your spirit. That's why it takes so long to heal.

–Anonymous

At this point on the healing path, it's natural to come up with questions as a thought pops into your head, or as you experience a moment of weakness when you aren't sure you can make it through. The most important of which may be, "How am I supposed to rebuild the person that I was before meeting my narcissistic abuser, when I don't remember that person anymore?"

It's a very real and heart-breaking question. Believe it or not, though, by having inquiries like this shows you are on the road to healing, and you don't even know it.

The person you were before your abuser came into your life was always there. They were merely pushed aside and ignored while you tended to the narcissist's needs. By asking the question above, or any of the other ones that may be on your mind (which we'll address shortly), it means that your inner self wants their voice heard again. Now that every space in your head isn't being occupied by another person's voice, your own needs are coming to the surface. So, it *is* possible to rebuild that person you were. You just need to build a stronger base upon which you construct them. And that's the focus of this chapter.

Firstly, we'll go over the stages of healing from narcissistic abuse. It's important to allow yourself to go through these so that everything is acknowledged and addressed in the most healthy way. If there are any loose threads not attended to, one tug will unravel all the hard work you're putting in. Within these stages, are things you absolutely must do (and not do) to solidify your recovery and healing path.

The second area to explore is creating your support networks. There are actually five different kinds of support networks to develop as your needs from those within each group differ slightly. These are individuals you may need to reach out during and after your decision to get out of your abusive relationship. Some of those people may have even been there before and during that experience. Others may be those you drew information or insight from to help you see the light of change. We'll talk about how to put them together, who to include, and who not to—and why their presence is so important to your healing and recovery.

The Stages of Healing, and the Importance of Support Networks

It's normal to go through different stages during the recovery and healing process, and it's also normal to move back and forth through stages as old feelings come up needing to be dealt with. There are no set rules in how you recover, or how long it should take.

The first stage—actively deciding to heal—you are already doing.

It may have stemmed from one specific event—one last straw that broke the camel's back—or an epiphany when you realize that enough is enough. Either way, you were tired of feeling awful all of the time and knew you had to do something to stop it. It's not unusual to feel stuck at this stage because *realizing* there's a problem and *taking action* to elicit change are different stages. Right when the light goes on that you need to feel better, that takes you to the next set of stages:

- **Removing all toxicity.** This isn't just removing the narcissist, it's discarding all the negativity they filled you with. That needs to go somewhere outside of and far away from you. It involves putting yourself into the shoes of the abuser, and seeing the world from their perspective. You've been doing this by gathering all the information you can about narcissism and understanding who they are and how they work. This isn't supposed to result in any empathy for them, but more seeing how they were able to get you to absorb their negativity so you can purge the toxicity from your body and mind. Their words won't disappear instantaneously, or at all in some cases. This is a difficult step, but a vital one that will bring you closer to healing.

- **Dealing with anxiety.** When the victim first gets away from their narcissist abuser, an outsider might think, "Well, there you go! The hardest part is over with!" Not true. The difficult part initially is having nothing else to tune out the chaos. Think about it: There has been someone constantly on you, putting you down, making you question everything you do, criticizing you, and eliciting debilitating anxiety. With only you to focus on— after not being a consideration for so long—it can be hard to adjust to. In fact, it can actually increase anxiety. This is when reaching out to support groups or those within your personal support network comes in handy. Don't be afraid to reach out for professional guidance too. This is not a time to deal with everything on your own.

- **Get angry.** Every recovery or healing plan has a stage where you need to allow yourself to feel every emotion you feel. Anger is a common one. Be angry at the abuser for what they did to you, be angry for not seeing it happen, or for not dealing with it when you did; be angry for how many different ways they infected you, and be angry that you're the one still suffering when they may have already gone on with their life completely guilt-free. This stage may come and go through other stages, and it's okay. It means you're winning.

- **Accept the truth so you can forgive *yourself*.** This could be a tough stage to pass through as well. After all, how can you forgive yourself for putting yourself in that situation, and staying with the toxic person? *That's* why you have to. The narcissist did and said terrible things that would result in everything always being your fault. They did this so often and so intensely that you absorbed that undeserved accountability into your soul. Forgiving yourself means you're fighting that mindset by saying, "It *wasn't* my fault. I didn't do anything wrong. I didn't know any better." This will stop self-blame, shame or guilt trying to wiggle its way back in, distracting you from your healing. Forgiveness is a powerful act, especially when you give it to yourself.

- **Set and stick to the no contact rule.** This was discussed earlier but that no contact boundary put up when you left has to remain iron-clad and not crossed–from either side. Do whatever you can, whatever humanly possible, to not succumb to their pleas to go back. They *won't* change. They *haven't* learned a thing by losing you. You *aren't* responsible for them. It could get ugly. They may even go behind your back and try making you look like the bad one. Let them. In the end, when you aren't fighting back or retaliating, they are the ones who look bad. Stay strong and on your path.

- **Don't get into a new relationship too soon.** Getting involved with a new person while you're in the process of healing from an abusive relationship isn't good for either of you. You still need to deal with everything you were put through, plus you may still be in a very vulnerable mindset to attract another narcissist. Give yourself time to heal before dipping your toe back in the pool.

- **Embrace your new life, and let go.** This is a step that will take quite a while to come to honestly and completely, but it will. Take the time you need to forgive yourself and replenish your soul with all the strength, beauty, and light it has been missing. Keep moving through your new life until you are able to let go, and finally have peace.

As you move through each of these stages, you need to have the comfort of knowing support is there to lean on for whatever you need. This is a time in life when you absolutely need to reach out, accept, and embrace any offers of support from trusted individuals. There are simply things you go through in life that you shouldn't have to face alone.

The Inside Scoop on Personal Support Networks

As it's probably becoming clearer, there are several factors involved in recovering successfully—and one of those things is having a good support network made up of friends, fellow survivors, faith confidantes, friends, family, and therapists. The number of people you have behind you isn't as important as the unconditional, loving support they can give to you. Not only does this support have a positive impact on mental health, they can help you through tough or weak moments, and ease feelings of isolation or loneliness.

Specifically, social networks offer the healing properties we lacked while with a person who had no connection to such behaviors and emotions, such as being cared for and about, and valued for who we are.

These networks are broken into four different groups based on what we turn to them for:

- **Appraisal:** Those in this branch of the support network are those we turn to for reminders of our strengths and attributes. They also help us stay in tune with our self-worth, self-esteem, and confidence.

- **Informational:** These people in the network are those who have knowledge of dealing with stressful situations or specific issues and where to get resources, insight, or extra help.

- **Instrumental:** Also called tangible, these are

people we can turn to for specific services such as a ride to an appointment, picking up a few items at the store, or even giving some monetary assistance when you need it. These acts of kindness are from the heart, unconditional, and with no expectation of "pay back". You need it, and they help you.

- **Emotional:** Of all support networks, those offering this kind of support may be the most needed. These are your huggers, tear-wipers, shoulders of steel, and continued nurture. They'd be the people who don't even need to say a word. They know their presence is sometimes all we need.

We'll always have certain people there for us no matter what the narcissistic ex tries to do during the break up. When a person slams another, and that person doesn't retaliate in any way, that says more about the person slamming than who they're directing it at. More importantly, there will be those who can see what you're going through even though you haven't said anything, and those are the supporters who will have deaf ears to the abuser. But it doesn't hurt to revamp your network periodically.

There will be those you thought would be there, but aren't. There are those who would be there, but may be going through their own tough times that they have to focus on. What you're going through at this moment may require you to reach out to a different set of support than you had before. You may be wondering, though: How are you supposed to reach out, to whom, and where? Then there are the residual effects of being in a highly abusive relationship that have impaired your trust in others, and yourself.

It may be reassuring to remember that there are many people who are also dealing with the after effects of trauma, they just need safe and approachable ways to find one another. One important point to make here is that while you're casting your social net out there, be cautious. We tend to attract those to us based on the vibe we put out. And when we're looking for those who have also gone through a narcissistic abusive relationship, one of two things could happen.

You'd either draw people to you who are at the same place you are, which isn't a bad thing—unless they unintentionally keep you there. When you have fellow survivors in your network, the goal should be embracing those who have been where you are and made it through to the end. These are people you aspire to be once you've traveled your recovery and healing path. Connecting with another person who hasn't fully reached that point is similar to two people who can barely keep their heads above water individually, while trying to keep each other afloat. The point is that if someone needs just as much support as you do, or even more, they aren't a person to get close to yet.

The other thing that could happen is that you could attract another narcissist. They seem to know when a person is at their most vulnerable so they can move in. This may be a person you can't detect right away because you haven't fully recovered from the last toxic relationship. You have the advantage, though—in that you are more knowledgeable and aware than you were initially—so if things start feeling familiar, run.

With all that said, here are a few safe ways to try

expanding your social network:

- **Adopt a pet.** Having a furry friend has so many benefits just on their own. They are loyal companions, they expect nothing from you but love and attention (and give it back), and they give you a reason to stay healthy and keep going. Plus, if you head out to the dog park, you can meet other pet owners.

- **Get a hobby.** This could either be one you put aside during your past relationship, or a brand new one you've always been interested in but never tried. Do some research and see if there are small groups in your community where you can paint or sculpt or even take up some kind of sporty hobby. Not only are you expanding your mind and keeping it busy in a healthy way, you will meet others with similar interests.

- **Connect online.** There are many Facebook, Instagram, or other social media groups, or even online groups created by community therapists. Modern technology makes it much easier to connect, especially on days you don't feel well enough to go outside your home. Again, be very cautious online as there are many predators in the world wide web world.

- **Volunteer**. This is a wonderful way to build your self-worth and self-esteem, by helping others in some way. A caution for this one is that occasionally those in high need may be drawn to those also in high need—even if you don't think you give off that vibe. Just be sure not to help or give at your own expense.

- **Reconnect with those already in your network.** You know they are your most loyal and dependable supporters in your times of need, but try contacting them just to talk or hang out with no trauma involved. Go for lunch or coffee, invite them over to watch a show or movie, or even go for a walk or mini adventure. These times are just as important for the supporter as they are for you, remembering that trauma aside, they are your friends and family, and you appreciate them.

Embracing the Mentally Tough Mindset to Stay on Track

Some of the most successful people embrace the mentally tough mindset. Considering that your mental health was the part of you most damaged in your narcissistic abusive relationship, finding the best way to heal it is essential. Being mentally tough isn't about arrogance or ego. It's more about the ability to face adversity as well-equipped as possible with a, "get up, dust off, and keep going" attitude. And you absolutely can achieve that.

Mental toughness is a part of your inner self that gives you the courage and strength to stick to your life plan and reach your goal. And when bumps come up, you see those as challenges to overcome rather than mountains of defeat. This isn't a quality that victims are guided towards in their healing process, but embracing a mentally tough mindset will strengthen you even more to keep going up the steps we've discussed throughout this book.

Here are some of the most common ways people

practice being mentally tough:

- **They are grateful.** To keep things in perspective, they focus on the good they have in their life, rather than dwelling on the hard times.

- **They keep their power close.** After having it taken from you in your toxic relationship, this is an important one to remember. Mentally tough people learn not to allow negative people to steal their power, and don't blame others for holding them back.

- **They only focus on what they can control.** This is also an important point for victims. When you're mentally tough, you only have control over what is within your power. Worrying about other things you can't control causes unnecessary stress and anxiety. Deal with what's in front of you, and let the rest go.

- **They have solid boundaries.** We've discussed the importance of boundaries. Mentally tough people refuse to allow others to chip away at their boundaries, and have no problem with saying no.

- **They aren't afraid to take safe risks.** Just as you were courageous enough to get away from your ex abuser, or each time you let your guard down a tiny bit to allow someone else in, a mentally tough person understands that it's healthy to take logical, calculated risks to better themselves.

- **Their past doesn't control their present or future.** It's a good thing to know the past is there, but it's not good to let it keep seeping into your present. Don't dwell on the past; let go of grudges and use it as a strength, rather than an excuse not to move forward.

- **They see mistakes as lessons.** We're human and we make mistakes, but we can't beat ourselves up for every poor choice or mistake. See them as an opportunity to learn new ways of doing things.

- **They don't compare themselves to others.** We're all individuals with different focuses and different goals. That means that our version of success is also different. You achieved tremendous success by making the decision to remove yourself from your abuser. That's something to be proud of and it's *your* success.

- **They're strong enough to be alone sometimes.** As we've discussed earlier, being alone after first getting out of an abusive relationship can be terrifying. But after time, you'll treasure alone time as it's when you can recharge your energy, reflect on current events in your life, or do some soul-searching.

- **They are perseverent.** This basically means that mentally tough people don't give up easily. They understand that what matters the most in life can take time, such as you becoming completely healed. They practice patience and persistence even when it feels like the odds are too high.

- **They are in tune with how their beliefs affect them.** As you already know, the inner talk we practice can help us along or rip us apart. As with mentally tough people, you need to be aware of the negative beliefs that hold you back from being where you want to be.

- **They are true to their values.** This revolves around your priorities and sticking to them, even though they may not be the most opted for in other people's opinion. Your values work side-by-side with your beliefs and you should always be courageous to stick with them.

- **They practice optimism.** This is an important point to embrace because coming out of an abusive relationship can leave you feeling rather pessimistic about life. The key is to have a realistic optimism where you don't listen to the pessimistic voice but you don't allow yourself to become overconfident and set yourself up for failure.

- **They put up with unpleasantness.** This means that if you reach out a tiny bit past your comfort zone, which will feel a little uncomfortable, try moving through it. It's a way to strengthen self-discipline and know that you'll be okay to venture out once in a while, despite all that you've gone through.

Many of these traits you probably already have, but

don't realize it. Weave the traits of a mentally tough person within your plan and you'll feel your inner self getting stronger with each thing you face.

In our final chapter, we're going to put all of the tips and strategies together to guide you on the rest of your healing pathway using the holistic approach.

Chapter 6

Putting It All Together

You don't ever have to feel guilty about removing toxic people from your life. It's one thing if a person owns up to their behavior and makes an effort to change. But if a person disregards your feelings, ignores your boundaries, and continues to treat you in a harmful way, they need to go.
–Daniell Koepke

To this point, you've learned many strategies to acknowledge that you're in a narcissistic abusive relationship. You learned how to strengthen your inner self to get out of the relationship and put together your plan of action to begin your recovery and healing. Now, we're going to put everything together in order to make sure you stay on that path.

The focus of this chapter is to prepare you to go from this point on. You'll arm yourself with more tools to make sure the relationships you embrace from here forward will be healthy, respectful, and loving. You're already halfway there by becoming closer to the inner self you'd forgotten about while you were with your narcissistic abuser. The key is keeping that self on the surface, reminding you of all the good in you that's worth fighting for, and that means severing the narcissist relationship cycle.

Another area to emphasize is living a more mindful life. The base of this view is to acknowledge the past, but not allowing it to seep into your present. It also means visualizing your future, but not looking so far ahead that you control the present to make that happen. The whole perception is to live each day to the fullest while understanding the past is only *part* of who we are, and the future will bring what we're meant to experience to guide us where we're supposed to be.

In the conclusion, we'll expand on the point of living mindfully by touching on some holistic approaches to add to your resource list. The holistic approach is a way to maintain the body, mind, and spirit view and treat the body as a whole, rather than separate components. The suggested practices are ways to strengthen the inner self in order to inspire you not to allow another person to drain it again.

Stopping the Narcissistic Relationship Abuse Cycle

The main lesson to take away from being free of a narcissistic relationship is that there are two people in the relationship, and the only one you have control over is you. It's frustrating to realize that the trait about us that attracted a narcissist is that we are sensitive, caring, and empathetic individuals. These are traits they don't have, and desperately want, and drain others of these traits inappropriately. And on the flip side, we are people who love taking care of others, so the narcissist benefits all around.

It isn't a bad thing to be a person who is sensitive to other people's needs. But when it is at your own expense and becomes an obvious unfillable need, it's a problem. Telling yourself that you just won't let it happen again isn't enough. It's in your nature to be kind and nurturing, and you shouldn't have to change that valuable trait because others take advantage of it. You simply need to stop trying so hard to please others and figure out exactly what *you* want from a relationship that you aren't getting.

That's where maladaptive relationship patterns stem from. In order to stop attracting toxic individuals who'll only take advantage of your beautiful traits, you first need to understand what you want and need. Only then will you be able to trust yourself enough to only allow those close to you who respect what your definition of acceptable and unacceptable treatment is. Here are a few questions to ask yourself:

- **What are my needs?** Are you trying so hard to take care of and help others because you didn't get enough of that yourself? What unfilled need are you trying to fill by putting other people's wants ahead of your needs? These are some tough questions to answer, but if you're helping to fill others' wants rather than their needs, you aren't doing it for the right reasons. Quite frankly, never give at your own expense.

- **Have I made my needs clear?** Are you in touch with your own needs? You should be able to express what your needs are, as well as how you feel. If the other person in the relationship either doesn't acknowledge your needs or even doesn't seem to care, that's the first sign that you're on another toxic path.

- **Are you helping the other person more than they try helping themselves?** This is a true eye-opener. If you have made things so comfortable for the other person that they aren't even trying to do things for themselves—that has to stop. Relationships are give and take, and if all the other person is doing is taking, they need to go.

- **Did you clarify what you expect?** If you have made your needs clear, did you also make it clear what your expectations are? When you've expressed your needs but the other person has made no effort in meeting them, they aren't meeting your expectations. We all deserve to have basic needs in any relationship met and if the other person isn't keeping up their end of the deal, they don't deserve you.

- **After trying everything, are your needs and feelings still being ignored?** Short and sweet, if you have tried everything possible to help make your side clear and they aren't even trying to understand your view—move on. Don't waste one more moment with a person who won't see past fulfilling their own wants and needs.

Embracing this mindset will change you and how you see others, which will lead you to finding healthier relationships. You'll become a person who won't settle for less than what is absolutely the best for you, and that's when people who appreciate those traits will push ahead of those who don't.

Stop Attracting Narcissists for Good

Now that your needs are clearly in place, and you have established how to make sure they are, we'll tackle the other components to strengthen you from getting into another narcissistic abusive relationship. Aside from what was discussed in the last section, there are five other things to consider when trying to solve the puzzle of not being able to ward of narcissists:

- **Did you have a narcissistic parent?** Of course, the first place looked at is whether this behavior is genetic or learned. There is some warrant, though, for considering what you learned from your caregivers or even other family members. You've informed yourself of the personality traits of a narcissist. The question to ask, then, do you see any of those same traits in either of your caregivers, other family members, friends, or a different ex? If so, some of the reason you keep finding yourself in the same toxic relationships is because they are familiar. Even at the most maladaptive, the familiar is more comfortable than venturing into something new.

- **Are you highly sensitive to other people's feelings?** This is empathy which, as discussed earlier, is a phenomenal trait. But narcissists seek this trait out in their partners and enjoy taking full advantage of their emotional generosity. Those sorts of people will never appreciate that trait in you, so sticking around waiting for gratitude will never be fulfilled.

- **Do you have low self-esteem?** The irony is that there are certain types of narcissists who actually attach themselves to other narcissists, or at least those who are stronger personality-wise, so they can enjoy the benefits without putting in any of the effort. But those with low self-esteem are much easier to manipulate and take advantage of, and they are easier to control. We've given many strategies to strengthen your self-esteem, and use it as a repellent against those toxic narcissists.

- **Do you stifle your own needs?** This was discussed in detail in the previous section, but will magnify the point. Denying yourself of your needs puts you in a very dangerous position, especially when dealing with a narcissist. They expect you to make *them* and *their* needs a priority, so denying or ignoring your own needs for theirs gives them exactly what they expect: A partner who has no emotional needs, who can exclusively focus on them. Once the toxic person sees you that way, they'll make it even more difficult for you to leave.

There are several other questions you can ask yourself, but you have most likely reached the level where you know how to stop the cycle from continuing.

Here are some refreshers:

1. **Solidify those boundaries.** This is a point we've resurfaced throughout this book but it's vital to keep it in full view. Your boundaries are your self-rules that prevent others from using you, taking advantage of you, and generally mistreating you. Know what you will and won't accept, create boundaries that honor those things, then stand behind them unquestioningly.

2. **Boost that self-confidence.** Your confidence and self-esteem work very closely together. Confidence is our belief in our abilities of what we

can do, and our self-esteem is our belief in ourselves and what confidence needs to move forward. Narcissists look for a partner who is low in both of these areas because they're easier to manipulate, control, and take advantage of. A narcissist will lose interest in a person they can't maneuver to their own advantage.

3. **Make values essential to you.** A narcissist can't fake something they neither understand nor connect with, so specify your values and morals, then try getting them to open up about theirs. Understanding these things means a person also must have empathy and the ability to view situations through other people's eyes. Knowing those things are important to you will turn them off pretty quickly.

4. **Be aware of the red flags.** You are already aware of who the narcissist is and the most prominent personality traits. You'd think that being involved with, and now away from them, you'd know another one a mile away. Being the deceptive people they are, they can slip under your highly

sensitive radar. They know how to behave differently in different scenarios they find themselves in, especially in regards to their treatment of their intimate partner. When the relationship is healthy, it will never emit a sense that something is amiss. Remember that your gut instincts are usually right so if you feel things aren't quite right, they most likely aren't.

5. **Only *you* control your behavior.** When another person even tries to control what you do, is overgenerous with their opinions, or gets irritated when you don't do what they tell you to—this screams narcissistic tactics you should turn away from. A person who wants to be with you would respect you for who you are and how you choose to be, *and* support you in those endeavors.

Rather than viewing this experience as a terrible event in your past, see it more as a challenge you overcame and allowed you to become an expert on the narcissistic personality. From that chaos came your expanded view on all the things you want and need for yourself, including all you embrace and also let go.

Living the Rest of Your Toxic-Free Life With Mindfulness

One aspect we've touched on earlier is how effective it is for your overall healing to embrace living mindfully. This is the ability to become aware of your whole self—physically, mentally, and spiritually—and accepting the now for everything it's worth. This mindset is particularly helpful for those who worry, are anxious, depressed, or who have lived through trauma—which is why it could be an invaluable strategy to add to your new life plan.

Since the road of recovery and healing is often bumpy and turbulent—one with periods of time when you take a few steps back—mindfulness helps to bring us back to the present and make us more aware of all that's around us. It guides us to see that life is full of gifts to be grateful for, and that living each day to the fullest makes life meaningful.

Mindfulness isn't a goal, it's a view to embrace, and there are a few techniques to try in practicing mindfulness:

- **Restructure our self-damaging thoughts.** What you've gone through shouldn't define who you are. We are absolutely our worst critics and, as we learned by being in a relationship with a toxic person, negative talk is much easier to believe than the good stuff. Every time those cutting, negative thoughts are stirred up, turn them around into more positive and uplifting words.

- **Teach yourself how to relax again.** A narcissistic partner has you feeling on edge, waiting for their beck and call, and dealing with their high wants and needs. Keeping the body in this state constantly is extremely unhealthy. One good strategy is being aware of the toxic, negative energy when it arises—demanding your attention—and just... stop. Don't respond immediately. Instead, sit still and become more aware of that demand rolling around in your head, then see yourself pulling away from it, or pushing it out of your way. Sit that way for several minutes, until you can go on to something else.

- **Be actively aware of your breathing.** The act of breathing goes far deeper than feeding the body the oxygen it needs. When faced with negativity or diversity, it's an effective way to re-channel your response and behavior. Deep breathing is good for your overall health and relaxes you so you can channel your emotions better. Deliberate and deep breathing is also the main component of meditation, which is also an excellent way to process thoughts and emotions before they come firing out. Once you can calm yourself down, you'll find meaning in all that you do.

- **Journaling.** Keeping a journal is a valuable way to channel your thoughts, emotions or whatever is affecting your overall mental functionality. Setting time aside each day to write out whatever is on your mind at that moment is healing, and a very safe way to express feelings. When you go over what you've written, you'll be able to see anything that is bothering you and why, then you can take proper action to put things back in sync.

The residual effects of ending a narcissistic abusive

relationship can stay with us for a long time. Even if we successfully get through all of the triggers, periods of self-doubt, moments of weakness wondering whether we made the right choice to leave; there will be times we slip back to those terrible times that nearly destroyed us. There may even be temptation to turn to maladaptive ways of coping just to silence those whispers from the past. Here's an analogy to keep close to you during those times.

See your past as being behind a glass wall. You can see it play out right there, but it can't get to you behind that wall. The problem is that the wall shouldn't be in front of you, informing your every instant of consciousness, it should be behind you. What's ahead of you is your future, which hasn't happened yet. And you can't allow it to share the present with you, because there isn't enough room for both. It's really hard not to let it be there because it can be so strong and powerful. But as you slowly progress through every baby step of your healing and recovery plan, that glass wall will gradually move around to where it should be, and stay: Behind you. You're allowed to look back at it occasionally. After all, what's behind that glass wall had a part in getting you to where you are right now. It loses its power once it cements into its place behind you, and in that moment you'll know you've made it through.

That's the main reason for living life mindfully, in the present. You need to be fully aware of your immediate environment and to make it safe against any invasion by your trauma behind that glass wall, and know how to accept things as they are today, so you can live the rest of your life in inner peace.

Chapter Summaries

There has been a great deal of information covered in this book. For ease of reference, the following is a summary of what was discussed in each chapter:

Chapter One: The chapter began with a description of a narcissist. Although the goal wasn't to create an empathetic view of the narcissist, there was an emphasis on arming oneself with as much knowledge as possible about what their common personality traits are, what different categories narcissists can be sorted into, and possible explanations of how they became that way. The more information the survivor has, the less of a threat the toxic person presents.

Chapter Two: The focus went deeper with a discussion of the different tactics a narcissist will use on their partners, complete with definitions and why they are so effective. At this point, the victim is figuring out that they are in a very unhealthy situation and plan to get out of it. The chapter ends with *do and don't* tips on dealing with narcissists.

Chapter Three: Once a victim understands who they're dealing with, they are now ready to see the signs of abuse. This chapter focuses on naming the abuse, calling out their abuser, and connecting with how this abuse is negatively affecting their health.

Chapter Four: The chapter starts with strategies on ways to begin the recovery process from narcissistic abuse. There is a list of strategies to begin the healing and recovery process by creating a recovery plan, which is the first step.

Chapter Five: A strong and reliable support network is vital to get through the abusive situation as well as for making it slowly down the lifepath to health. The chapter discusses how to put together support networks, the different types of networks based on what's needed, and prevention strategies to avoid being lured back to the abuser. The chapter ends with a discussion on mental toughness and how to draw from it to stay on the healing path.

Chapter Six: All discussions and points in each chapter are brought together with insight on how to ensure that any future relationships are healthy ones, and how to live mindfully—in the present.

Conclusion: This is a summary of the book. There's also a detailed list for various holistic practices to incorporate into the recovery plan. Finally, there is a list of lessons that victims of narcissistic abuse have learned, and can take forward as they learn to love themselves and, hopefully, feel comfortable connecting with another partner down the path.

Conclusion

You may not control all the events that happen to you, but you can decide not to be reduced by them.

–Maya Angelou

In the beginning of this book, we made it clear that the focus is less on bringing empathy for the narcissists we share the world with but more for their victims who blindly move into a relationship with them. Although we included the basics of who a narcissist is, possible reasons they became the way they are, and the most common tactics they practice on their partners. The main focus is on offering insight, strategies, and tips for those who have removed themselves from a narcissistic abusive relationship.

The struggles you faced back then—and the perseverance it will take to remain on your healing path—won't end when you close this book. The points and pearls of wisdom will be here to review, to uplift you, to remind you of all good you're doing, and to be a silent cheerleader that will remain with you until "I'm healing" becomes "I'm healed".

For the ending of this book, we're going to provide a list of various holistic therapies you can feel free to look into. These practices are included here as additional resources that will keep you grounded and focused as you celebrate your new lifepath. They follow the theme repeated throughout the book of treating the whole self, not just the separate components of body, mind, and spirit. Remember that before entering any form of therapy–holistic or traditional–to discuss the practice in detail with your primary health care provider. They will know what methods you'll receive the greatest benefits from, or which combination of practices may work better. That is a precaution not to take lightly.

As a final applause, we'll share lessons that, hopefully, you've learned after leaving the toxic relationship behind you and having the courage to want better for yourself. You should be proud of all you've done because there are those still where you were. Perhaps, one day, you can take all the wisdom you possess and advocate for those whose voices can't be heard over the one speaking over them. That's powerful.

Holistic Practices 101 for Overall Health

Although holistic therapy is a good addition to anyone's goal of optimal health, it's especially beneficial to those who live with anxiety, depression, high stress, and trauma. These are all states of mind that throw the entire body out of whack, which impairs our ability to respond in an effective way. Keeping the body in a constant state of fear, fight, or response mode can cause negative health effects in several of the body's functions.

There are many types of holistic therapies, all of which follow the premise to realign the energies in the body so the individual can bring their body back down to a resting state, and help the body's energies get back into sync.

The following are the most common types of these therapies most effective in dealing with the body-mind-brain connection, particularly trauma:

1. **Breathwork:** This may be one of the first ones to try as being in tune with breathing is the base for many of the practices. It's a way to control, and be more consciously aware, of our breathing. It's beneficial for those who have gone through trauma as it helps to regulate the nervous system (e.g. heart rate, breathing, nervousness, etc.). Other benefits include increasing lung capacity, decreasing anxiety symptoms, and better sleep.

2. **Meditation and yoga:** These practices are also good for those living with the after effects of trauma. Both of them focus on the importance of breathing. Meditation, though, returns the mind to and keeps it in the present, while yoga reconnects the mind-body-spirit through specific poses geared to the individual's specific needs.

3. **Stress management:** The individual is guided through putting together a plan to deal with stress head-on, rather than allowing it to build up. Each plan will look different for each person as our stressors, the intensity of them, and our tolerance level for coping with them are also different. But managing stress effectively can greatly reduce negative impacts to our overall health.

4. **Somatic experiencing:** For those who have PTSD, or another form of trauma, this is a way to focus on bodily reactions to the event before addressing the psychological symptoms. For many survivors, the symptoms are so unpleasant they block any other form of therapy to deal with the actual traumatic event. Connecting with how that event made the body feel, and work through those emotions, puts a person in a stronger state to deal with the trauma in a healthier way.

5. **Cognitive behavioral therapy (CBT):** This practice helps us analyze how our thoughts and emotions have a huge impact on our reactions and behaviors. The main goal is to have the individual

recognize the patterns of their thoughts and emotions, then restructure them in a more positive and effective way. It should be noted that this form of treatment doesn't focus on past events, but more on how to cope better in the present. This wouldn't be an ideal form of therapy for a person wanting to dig to the deepest roots of their behavior.

6. **Acupuncture:** For centuries, this practice has been used in Chinese medicine as a way to realign disconnected energies in the body through the use of inserting needles at specific points in the body. It's been known to help with pain, anxiety, and many other conditions.

7. **Chiropractic:** Practitioners in this approach focus on strengthening and stimulating the brain-spine connection and healing physiological and emotional struggles through a series of spinal adjustments.

8. **Massage:** This has slowly become one of the more common practices to turn to for coping with

the bodily symptoms of stress, anxiety, and trauma. The muscles are often tense when the body is under high stress, and massage can help ease pain, relieve body stress, or realign disconnected energies.

9. **Tai Chi:** The practice is like moving through meditation. Also a Chinese centuries-old form of low-impact martial arts, combining the benefits of breathwork, motion, and focus.

10. **Grounding:** For those living with PTSD, traumatic memories, dissociation and anxiety, this practice helps with the flashbacks or triggers of terrifying memories by helping the individual to focus on the present rather than succumbing to the trigger pull of the past.

11. **Cranial sacral therapy (CST):** This relieves tension and compression in the head, neck, and spine—places of stress and tension for many individuals. For many people, relieving discomfort in these areas can ease one into dealing with what's causing the symptoms.

12. **Reiki:** This is a Japanese practice that focuses on the realignment of the body's energies, as well as to unblock any energy paths that have been blocked during times of prolonged stress and trauma.

13. **Sound healing:** This practice relies on the sounds and vibrations of instruments or *singing bowls*. The vibrations affect brain waves as well as balance the chakra systems—which are energy centers associated with specific organs and systems in the body.

14. **Guided imaging therapy (GIT):** This practice focuses on positive imagery in order to bring the body back down to a calm and relaxed state of mind to work through any negative thoughts or emotions that may be ignored or repressed.

15. **Emotional freedom technique (EFT):** Also known as "mind acupuncture", involves tapping on main energy pathways that help to refocus physical symptoms resulting in the healing of cognitive, emotional, and physical levels.

As you can see there are many to choose from based on your needs, your tolerance level for touch, and the severity of your symptoms. The holistic approach is an umbrella of practices to incorporate into your healing plan you already have in place. And to reiterate the earlier point, don't begin any practice without getting the go-ahead from your primary healthcare provider.

10 Lessons You Learned After Surviving Narcissistic Abuse

After all you've gone through and worked through during your journey in this book, your job should now be focused on healing. As already discussed, you shouldn't search out another relationship until you are on stronger, steadier ground. But you now have all the tools you need to move into a healthier relationship with a person who treats you the way you deserve to be treated.

In a strange way, the narcissist actually taught you a few valuable things. They showed you all of the negatives you shouldn't tolerate as well as guided you to a clearer view of your needs, wants, and values, as well as what your new definition of love is.

With all of that in mind, we'll leave you with the ten lessons we hope you've learned after getting out of your abusive narcissistic relationship:

- **You aren't fooled by false flattery.** You now know that all the love-bombing, attention, gifts, and other promises aren't given from the person's heart, but more as ways to lure you in closer and for you to adore them. Because of that, you're able to see the difference between true intentions and false flattery.

- **You appreciate "slow and steady" over "fast and furious".** In a nutshell, a narcissist doesn't want to waste time with all the "get to know each other inside and out" stuff before making any serious plans for the future together. They want what they want *now*. You see the red flag immediately and know that any relationship with you is worth the wait.

- **There is value in being accountable.** You know

that a narcissist would rather see another person go down for their mistakes than to take onus for them. It takes a much more mature person to not only own up to their mistakes but to learn from them, including fixing what they can.

- **You appreciate the importance of a life outside a relationship.** You may not have fully appreciated having hobbies, interests, or even connections outside of what you had in your narcissistic relationship. They never saw the need for such things when you could put all of your focus and energy on them. Having these things in your life is a way of focusing on your needs, which you weren't allowed to do previously. A new person in your life will appreciate and support your needs.

- **It made you stronger than you believed.** You know that being in a toxic relationship is difficult, and that ending it and having to redesign your life is even more difficult. But you did it. The strength is from taking all of the negatives you faced and turning them into learning blocks from which to blossom and grow.

- **You know the toxic relationship isn't a sign of weakness.** If anything, realizing that toxicity and removing yourself from it are signs of strength. When you think about it, the narcissist wasn't feeding on your weaknesses, but on your strengths of empathy, kindness, and caring nature. These are traits that a new person will both treasure and value.

- **You learned that partners celebrate either other's successes.** Narcissists don't mind if their partner is successful as long as their toes aren't being stepped on. They don't tolerate a significant other being in *their* spotlight, and punish mercilessly for doing it. You know now that a supportive partner will celebrate every accomplishment and achievement right alongside you, and never guilt you for those things.

- **You know to have firm boundaries.** Not only do narcissists have no boundaries, they don't respect them. How are they supposed to respect something they don't even understand? Through having your boundaries constantly destroyed and crossed, you know the importance of setting boundaries, ensuring they are iron-clad, and making sure that no one crosses them.

- **You understand that being emotionally vulnerable is strength.** Narcissists consider showing emotions or any form of emotional vulnerability a sign of weakness. It takes a much braver and stronger person to be willing to show vulnerability to another. It shows trust, openness, and a desire to go deeper into a relationship. There is no weakness in any of those.

- **You realize you can't make everyone happy.** One of the hard lessons you learned is that narcissists are impossible to truly please—even though they demand your constant effort to. They want perfection which doesn't exist in the real world. Human beings are all flawed in some way; it's what makes us each unique. You've learned that your happiness is above everything else, and that a person who wants to be with you needs to be on board with that premise, just as you'd be for them.

We hope that you've learned strategies and tips that will keep you on your healing path. Be proud of who you are, how hard you've worked to be who you are, and your strength. Your life has a new purpose.

Thank You

Before you leave, I'd just like to say, thank you so much for purchasing my book.

I spent many days and nights working on this book so I could finally put this in your hands.

So, before you leave, I'd like to ask you a small favor.

Would you please consider posting a review on the platform? Your reviews are one of the best ways to support indie authors like me, and every review counts.

Your feedback will allow me to continue writing books just like this one, so let me know if you enjoyed it and why. I read every review and I would love to hear from you. Simply visit the link below to leave a review.

To leave a review simply scan the QR code below or go to Amazon.com, go to "Your Orders" and then find it under "Digital Orders".

Scan the QR Code Below to Leave a Review:

References

Beard, C. (June, 2021). *6 tips for increasing social support.* (2021). Psychology Today. https://www.psychologytoday.com/us/blog/lab-real-world/202106/6-tips-increasing-social-support

Cuncic, A. (2021). *Effects of narcissistic abuse.* Verywell Mind. https://www.verywellmind.com/

Dodgson, L. (2018, February 11). Here's how to stop an argument with a narcissist. Business Insider; Insider. https://www.businessinsider.com/how-to-stop-argument-with-narcissist-2018-2

Dodgson, L. (October 22, 2018). *How to leave a narcissist in 14 steps.* Insider; Insider. https://www.insider.com/how-to-leave-a-narcissist-in-14-steps-2018-10#dont-rush-into-anything-17

Fielding, S. (September 4, 2017). Mindbodygreen. https://www.mindbodygreen.com/articles/how-to-stop-attracting-narcissists-and-abusers

Gregory, C. (October 25, 2021). *Narcissistic personality disorder (NPD): Causes, symptoms, treatment.* (2021, October 25). Psycom.net - Mental Health Treatment Resource since 1996. https://www.psycom.net/personality-disorders/narcissistic/

References

Lancer, D. (2018, May 22). *Confronting narcissistic abuse*. Psych Central; Psych Central. https://psychcentral.com/lib/confronting-narcissistic-abuse#5

Maggie. (February 19, 2018). *Blueprint for narcissistic abuse recovery*. https://narcwise.com/2018/02/19/blueprint-for-narcissistic-abuse-recovery/

Mason, M. (January 17, 2020). *Pathways family coaching*. Narcissistic Coping Mechanisms - Pathways Family Coaching. https://pathwaysfamilycoaching.com/narcissistic-coping-mechanisms/

Mayer, B A.. (February 9, 2022). *Holistic therapy: Treating body, mind, and spirit for whole person healing*. Healthline; Healthline Media. https://www.healthline.com/health/mental-health/holistic-therapy#types

Morin, A. (June 8, 2016). 18 habits of mentally strong people. Inc.com; Inc. https://www.inc.com/amy-morin/18-things-mentally-strong-people-do.html

Neuharth, D. (2019). 10 things not to do with narcissists. Psychology Today. https://www.psychologytoday.com/us/blog/narcissism-demystified/201907/10-things-not-do-narcissists

Parker, M. (September 7, 2020). 8 stages of healing after escaping narcissistic abuse. Her Way. https://herway.net/8-stages-healing-escaping-narcissistic-abuse/

Pomerace, M. (March 12, 2021). 7 crucial things no one tells you about recovering from narcissistic abuse. The Candidly. https://www.thecandidly.com/2019/7-crucial-things-no-one-tells-you-about-recovering-from-narcissistic-abuse

Steines, S. (2018, May 7). *Common questions asked by people healing from narcissistic abuse* . GoodTherapy.org Therapy Blog. https://www.goodtherapy.org/blog/common-questions-asked-by-people-healing-from-narcissistic-abuse-0507184

Stow, C.V. (September 12, 2019). 5 holistic therapies that will clear all of your emotional blockages pronto. ELLE; ELLE. https://www.elle.com/uk/life-and-culture/culture/g28862031/holistic-therapies-for-emotional-blockages/

Teller, S, E. (October 21, 2020). *Mindfulness techniques that work.* Sara Teller. https://sarateller.com/mindfulness-techniques-that-work/

Wade, D. (January, 2022). *12 signs you've experienced narcissistic abuse (plus how to get help).* Healthline; Healthline Media. https://www.healthline.com/health/narcissistic-victim-syndrome#self-blame

Ward, D. (2013). *Stop the narcissist relationship cycle.* Psychology Today. https://www.psychologytoday.com/ca/blog/sense-and-sensitivity/201310/stop-the-narcissist-relationship-cycle

Watson, S. (2020). *10 lessons you learn after dating a narcissist | EliteSingles.* EliteSingles. https://www.elitesingles.ca/en/mag/single-life/relationship-with-narcissist?CID=CA_SEM_1_12461589532_117962983589_502236728608&gclid=CjwKCAiA1JGRBhBSEiwAxXblwfL3B7s1yFIym-sqpVQqoAnD8HHGGxGcjzbh3uhTQ3BoQQy-Sn1STBoCv2QQAvD_BwE